Contents

Words in **bold** are in the glossary on page 23.

Discover | Share

On Th RAW Road

Deborah Chancellor

W

FRANKLIN WATTS

Going places

We all need **transport** to help us get to where we want to go. There are many different kinds of **vehicle** on the road.

Some vehicles take people and others carry **goods.**

About this book

The **Discover and Share** series enables young readers to read about familiar topics independently. The books are designed to build on children's existing knowledge while providing new information and vocabulary. By sharing this book, either with an adult or another child, young children can learn how to access information, build word recognition skills and develop reading confidence in an enjoyable way.

Reading tips

➡ Begin by finding out what children already know about the topic. Encourage them to talk about it and take the opportunity to introduce vocabulary specific to the topic.

➡ Each image is explained through two levels of text. Confident readers will be able to read the higher level text independently, while emerging readers can try reading the simpler sentences.

➡ Check for understanding of any unfamiliar words and concepts. Inexperienced readers might need you to read some or all of the text to them. Encourage children to retell the information in their own words.

➡ After you have explored the book together, try the quiz on page 22 to see what children can remember and to encourage further discussion.

There are lots of ways to travel on the road.

Pedal power

Riding a bike is a good way to get around. Some people race on bicycles, or cycle off-road.

You can ride over steep and rough ground on a mountain bike. It has tough, wide tyres.

Some people race on their bikes. This bike has strong tyres.

Hot wheels

A motorbike is a bike with an **engine**.
Little scooters can zip through traffic.
Bigger motorbikes are specially made
for longer trips. Other motorbikes
race on tracks.

There are lots of kinds of motorbike. This motorbike is made for long trips.

Car crazy

Cars come in all sorts of different shapes and colours. Most cars run on **petrol**, but some use **electricity**.

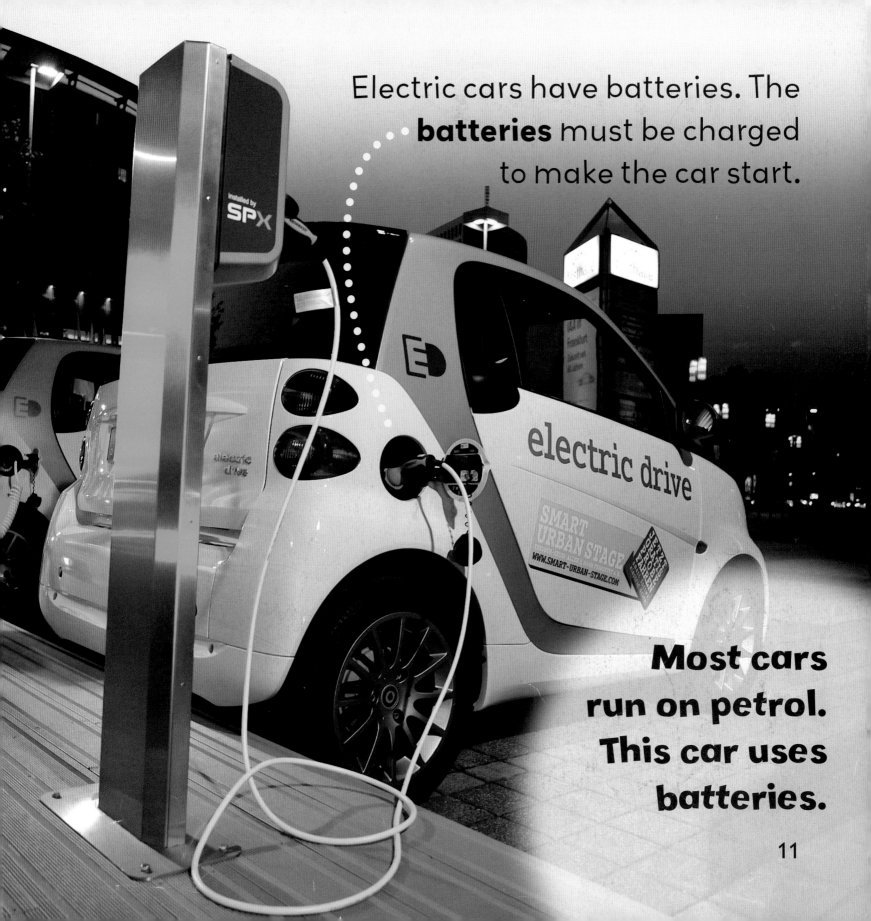

Electric cars have batteries. The **batteries** must be charged to make the car start.

Most cars run on petrol. This car uses batteries.

Speed racer

Motor racing is a top sport.
These cars go very fast.

Motor racing is a popular sport, with millions of fans. Some of the world's fastest cars hit speeds of up to 400 kilometres per hour.

The engines of racing cars wear out after just two hours on the race track!

Off to work

Vans are used to move people or things from one place to another. They have a front seat, with space behind.

Vans **deliver** anything from food and drink to letters and boxes.

Vans can move people or things.
This van carries boxes.

Big truck

Trucks transport goods on the road. Some of them are very big and heavy. A truck with eighteen wheels weighs about forty tons. That is the same as sixteen cars!

**Trucks carry goods on the road.
Some trucks are very big.**

On the buses

Coaches take people on trips. These buses have lots of seats.

Different kinds of bus are used for different trips. **Coaches** have plenty of seats for passengers. Tour buses have open tops, so people ······· can see the sights.

City tram

There are trams in cities all over the world. They run on tracks in the road and get their power from electricity **cables**.

Trams don't get stuck in traffic. They always arrive on time!

This tram runs on a track in the road. It is always on time.

Quiz

1. What is a motorbike?

2. Which kind of car runs on batteries?

3. Why do tour buses have open tops?

4. What kind of power do trams use?

Glossary

batteries a store of electricity

cables thick wires

coach a big bus with lots of seats that is used to make longer journeys

deliver to take goods to a place

electricity energy that is used to make heat and light and to power machines

engine the motor that powers a vehicle

goods things that people eat, drink or use

motor racing car racing

petrol a kind of fuel that is used to drive vehicles

transport a way of being taken from one place to another

vehicle a means of transporting people or things

Answers to quiz:
1. A bike with an engine.
2. Electric.
3. So people can see the sights.
4. Electricity.

Index

This edition copyright ©
Franklin Watts 2014

Franklin Watts
338 Euston Road
London
NW1 3BH

Franklin Watts Australia
Level 17/207 Kent Street
Sydney
NSW 2000

ISBN 978 1 4451 3648 6
Library ebook ISBN 978 1 4451 2498 8
Dewey number: 629.2

A CIP catalogue record for this book is
available from the British Library.

Series Editor: Julia Bird
Series Advisor: Karina Law
Series Design: Basement68

Picture credits: Adisa/Shutterstock: 5. Bikeworldtravel/Shutterstock: 19,
22bl. Candy Box Images/Shutterstock: 15. Raphael Christinat/
Shutterstock: 3c, 7. Culturaleyes-AusG52/Alamy: 18. Chad Elhers/Alamy:
3b, 21. hfng/Shutterstock: 10, 23. javarman/Shutterstock: front cover.
Lcro77/Dreamstime: 11, 22tr. m-images/Alamy: 1, 9.
Majeczka/Dreamstime: 14. Natursports/Shutterstock: 3t, 8, 13, 22tl.
NK/Shutterstock: 4. Tatiana Popova/Shutterstock: 12.
Pressmaster/Shutterstock: 6. Paul Ridsdale/Alamy: 17.
saswell /Shutterstock: 20, 22br. Vibrant Image Studio/Shutterstock: 2, 16.

Printed in China

Franklin Watts is a division of
Hachette Children's Books,
an Hachette UK company.
www.hachette.co.uk